Philosophical RE

Introduction

Religion might be jealous of philosophy for its cool head, but philosophy might be jealous of religion for the millions of adherents it has. RE needs both philosophy and religion to be part of its field of enquiry. Philosophy (the love of wisdom) is fundamentally about asking and answering questions about 'the world, the universe and everything'. Philosophical thinking provides frameworks through which questions of individual and corporate identity and meaning are explored. It addresses what it means to be human (individually and corporately), the nature of existence (past, present and future) and considers implications for living (morally and ethically). Religious Education (RE) is likewise fundamentally about enabling pupils to ask and answer 'ultimate' questions of what it means to be human and what it means to be them within the context of the answers and further questions that religious belief and practice raise. Secular philosophies offer alternatives to religious belief, and addressing similarities and differences between the two can be fruitful ground for religious/ philosophical thinking in RE. Ours therefore is also a very 'philosophical' subject and the experiences and opportunities we provide for pupils should engage them with the skills and attitudes towards their learning that allow them to ask, and seek answers to, probing questions based on logical and analytical thinking as well as focused on creativity and problem-solving.

In this resource some key RE and philosophical questions are explored and activities exemplified that can be adapted across different ability- and age-groups, to develop skills so that philosophical thoughtful RE is encouraged. Other books in this series from RE Today offer further similar stimuli: *Thoughtful RE* (April 2007), *Spiritual RE* (April 2008) and *Ethical RE* (January 2009).

Lat Blaylock
Series Editor

with thanks to Pamela Draycott

Contents

Page	Section
2	RE and philosophy: asking big questions: FAQs
5	What is real? How do we know? What do we mean by reality? Lat Blaylock
10	Does believing in God make people good? Ed Pawson
15	Why evil and suffering? Rosemary Rivett
20	What is God like? Victoria Ikwuemesi
24	The community of philosophical enquiry: how can RE benefit? Pat Hannam
29	Is it true? How do you know? Some models of philosophical and religious truth Lat Blaylock and Victoria Ikwuemesi

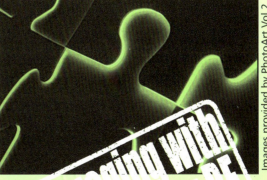

RE and philosophy: asking big questions: FAQs

1. What is philosophy and how does it relate to religion?

Philosophy: the love and pursuit of wisdom by intellectual means and moral self-discipline. The critical analysis of fundamental assumptions or beliefs. Investigation of the nature, causes and principles of reality, knowledge and values, based on logical reasoning.

For some, philosophy is what religion is really about. Religions are seen as the treasure chests by which human understandings of wisdom and reality are passed from one generation to the next. This view of religions is contested by others, who see faith as much more encompassing and holistic than philosophy. But if religion does not ask and pursue philosophical questions about truth, goodness, the nature of things, life's meanings and purposes, then it might collapse into unreasoned superstition.

Here is a clue to why this series of booklets from RE Today includes one about philosophical RE: since RE is about religion, then a part of RE must address philosophical questions and the ways in which religions respond to them.

2. Should RE tackle philosophical issues more?

In the last decade, RE has been getting more philosophical: big questions, ultimate issues are addressed by excellent RE teachers with younger and younger pupils. The time RE spends on analysing beliefs has generally increased. RE teachers don't, themselves, need to be philosophers, but they do need to enable pupils to think, reasonably, about religion, truth, goodness and meaning. This far at least, all RE teachers need philosophical tools such as those we present in this book. It's also worth noting that, compared to religion, philosophy is the pursuit and interest of a tiny minority. Religions are rather good at gathering and inspiring their adherents to the pursuit of truth in community.

3. Can philosophical enquiry methods improve standards in RE?

- Yes: If a teacher introduces more philosophical RE, emphasising the place of argument, reasonableness, questioning, looking at evidence and exploring questions of meaning, purpose and truth, then pupils' motivation may be improved by the connections the material makes to their lives and interests.

- The rigour of thinking in RE may be improved by the development of sharper study methods.

- Pupils' understanding of religions can improve from thinking that 'religious people are funny, and do funny things in funny clothes', to the realisation that religions are ways in which humanity grapples with life's mysteries and meanings, and that anyone can learn from the insights of religions, whether they belong within the faith community or locate themselves beyond it.

- Standards can be raised by a more philosophical RE.

Frequently asked questions (FAQs)

4. What are 'ultimate questions'?

Hans Kung, the great German theologian of the twentieth century, asks the ultimate questions like this:

What can we know? Why is there anything at all, why not nothing? Where does humanity come from, and where do we go? Why is the world as it is? What is the ultimate reason and meaning of all reality? What ought we to do? Why do what we do? Why and to whom are we finally responsible? What deserves contempt, and what love? What is the point of loyalty? Friendship? Suffering? Sin? What really matters for humanity? What may we hope? Why are we here? What is it all about? What is there left for us – death, making everything pointless at the end? What will give us courage for life, and what for death?

(Kung, *On being a Christian*, Fount 1978, pp.75–6).

An RE classroom would surely be enhanced if these questions were all over the walls, with learners' answers and suggestions all over them. The idea of 'ultimacy' is important here, because it draws our attention to the nature of these questions: they are answered in different profound ways. They are not contingent or material questions, but upon the answers we choose or give to them our whole lives may turn. In that sense, ultimate questions matter more than the questions of mere science, mathematics or history.

5. What is philosophical RE? Content, method, skills?

RE is philosophical when its **content** concentrates on questions of meaning, purpose and truth, and the ways religions address these questions.

RE is philosophical when its **methods** use argument, reason, interpretation, clarification of terms and analysis to explore its subject matter.

RE is philosophical when learners develop the **skills** of philosophical enquiry for themselves, and apply them to religious materials. The particular skills of learning from religion and the personal search for meaning include the ability to handle questions with increasing discernment and profundity. The opposite of this is when pupils develop the skills of a photocopier – to reproduce accurately what they are given.

6. What is 'Philosophy for Children' (P4C)? How can it enhance learning in RE?

P4C is, as its name suggests, a philosophical approach to developing thinking in children and young people, developed in the USA by Matthew Lipman in the 1960s. The emphasis is on **questioning** and **reasoning**. An issue or question is identified which might be solved or elucidated through discussion by the whole group (**the community of enquiry**). The teacher is in the role of the facilitator and supports or challenges the discussion and reasoning as appropriate. Patricia Hannam's article on pages 24–28 explores this method in RE in depth.

3

7. What can the RE department do?

Some **self-evaluation questions** to ask in relation to **philosophical RE**:

Grade your work like this: 1 = Outstanding, 2 = Good, 3 = Satisfactory and 4 = Inadequate, and supplement each question with this one: How do we know and what do we need to do to target further improvement?

- How well do we, through our RE **curriculum content** and **planning, address philosophical questions** of **meaning** and **purpose**, drawing on the **insights** of different **'religious'** and **'secular'** world views? How effective are we at providing opportunities that allow pupils to address philosophical **methods of enquiry** to support their learning in RE (framing, asking and answering questions)?

- How good are we at supporting pupils in developing **skills** to encourage philosophical thinking such as analytical, evaluative and logical thought processes (skills)? How well do we encourage pupils to **think and reflect upon their thinking** (metacognition)?

- How good are we at encouraging pupils to be **creative problem-solvers** in RE through the **experiences and opportunities** we provide for them (creativity)?

8. Where can I find out more?

A first and crucial reference point for RE is the statutory locally agreed syllabus, faith community guidelines, or equivalent, e.g. *Religious and Moral Education Guidelines*, Scotland (www.ltscotland.org.uk/5to14). Also, any non-statutory guidelines published by local SACREs and/or faith community bodies. The information provided here draws significantly from the following:

- ***Non-Statutory National Framework for RE*** (QCA 2004) and example unit of work on science and religion for English Year 9 pupils (QCA 2007) – www.qca.org.uk

- **SAPERE and Philosophy for Children**: www.sapere.org.uk

- **UNESCO's intersectorial philosophical enquiry strategy** (2006):

www.unesdoc.unesco.org/images/0014/001452/145270e.pdf

- Joanna Haynes, ***Children as Philosophers: Learning Through Enquiry and Dialogue in the Primary Classroom*** 2nd revised edn, (Routledge 2008) ISBN 978-0-415-44680-8 – a book with a primary focus but with useful insights for the secondary phase also; Susanna R Hookway, ***Questions of Truth: Developing Critical Thinking Skills in Secondary Religious Education*** (RMEP 2004) ISBN 9781851753260; Brenda Watson and Penny Thompson, ***The Effective Teaching of Religious Education***, 2nd revised edition (NYP 2006) ISBN 9781405824101.

- **From RE Today Publications,** in the series Developing Secondary RE: *Evil and Goodness, Codes for Living, Questions about God*, and *Science and Religion*.

- **Broadcast resources:** *Curriculum Bites RE* (Series 1, 2003, Series 2, 2005) has lots of relevant materials including 'To die for…', 'Miracles', 'A short religious history of…' 'Is God real?' and 'The big questions'. Details from www.retoday.org.uk

What is real? How do we know? What do we mean by reality?

For the teacher

This part of the booklet uses questions about reality to enable learning from religion, particularly with reference to Christianity, Buddhism and Hindu traditions. While this work may fit well with students and syllabuses in the 14–16 age range (it connects with some GCSE and Standard Grade topics), it is also usable with higher-achieving pupils in the 12–14 age group. The aims of the work are to enable pupils to:

- Apply some simple philosophical methods to the questions: What is real? How do we know? What do we mean by reality?
- Understand some ways in which Christians, Buddhists and Hindus explain their vision of reality.
- Describe and explain their own views and questions about the nature of the real.

Achievements

Pupils can demonstrate achievement at levels 5–7 in these activities, if they can say 'yes' to some of these 'I can...' statements.

Level 5: I can...

- Explain two different religious ideas about the meaning of 'reality' and express my own views using religious and philosophical terminology well.

Level 6: I can...

- Interpret the ideas of religion and philosophy about reality for myself, expressing insights of my own into the diverse views studied.

Level 7: I can...

- Use the methods of philosophy to give coherent accounts of different understandings of reality, drawing balanced conclusions of my own.

Three 'reality' activities

1. **A questionnaire about reality** This is a good starter activity, and can be developed into some philosophical discussion work. Pupils who answer with As and Bs to questions 2, 4, 8, 19 and 20 probably go for D and E on questions like 1, 9 or 12. Ask pupils which are the most interesting questions and why. For these ones, take class votes and discussion comments. Ask high-achieving pupils to devise a similar questionnaire of their own.

2. **Stories of the real** The four stories on pages 7 and 8 can be copied for classroom use. The activities outlined to go with them enable pupils to think afresh about the ways they use the concept 'reality'. While only one of the stories is explicitly religious ('The Enlightened Chicken'), they all relate to religious views of the world. For example, a Christian might interpret Plato's parable like this: The prisoners are those who have never seen the truth about God. The freed prisoner is enlightened by the Holy Spirit to God's real purposes. The other prisoners resent his new insight, and kill him as they killed Jesus before him.

3. **The 'maze of ideas'** on page 9 enables learners to work in a highly structured speaking and listening activity that explore a variety of ideas, religious and philosophical, about reality. The format of this can be adapted for lower-achieving pupils. There is an example of this on the RE Today website: www.retoday.org.uk

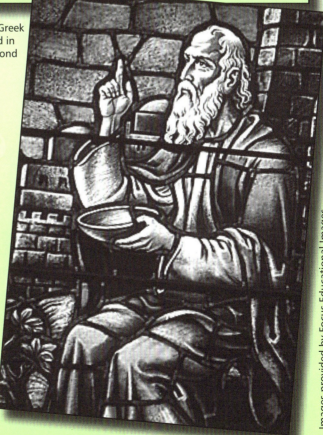

Socrates, father of Greek philosophy, believed in a real world far beyond this one.

Images provided by Focus Educational Images

What is real? How do you know?

This questionnaire will help you to get clear your own ideas about what is real. Complete it alone, then discuss the answers with two partners in a group of three.

Get real

Agree strongly = A,
Uncertain, unsure = C
Disagree totally = E

1.	Dreams are real.	A B C D E
2.	I only believe in what I can see, touch or hear. My senses tell me what is real.	A B C D E
3.	I think 'reality' is impossible to define and describe: how can we know?	A B C D E
4.	Dreams are real, but not in the same way that 'real life' is real.	A B C D E
5.	Maybe I am just a part of your dreams. We can't prove this one way or the other.	A B C D E
6.	What most people mean by 'real life' is just their own point of view.	A B C D E
7.	Love is real.	A B C D E
8.	God is not real.	A B C D E
9.	The human mind is real. We can't see it, and we can't touch it, but it's there, somehow, in the brain. But it's not the same as the brain.	A B C D E
10.	If angels were real, we still would not be able to see them.	A B C D E
11.	I think that human emotions – like shame, guilt, love and pleasure – are more important and real than some so-called material realities.	A B C D E
12.	Virtual reality has become real.	A B C D E
13.	The world wide web is real.	A B C D E
14.	If we are automatic robots who have been programmed to think we are free people, then we wouldn't be able to tell.	A B C D E
15.	The material world is one kind of reality. The worlds of soul, thoughts, spirituality and emotions are real too, but in a different way.	A B C D E
16.	Reality TV is about as unreal as it's possible to get. Real life is nothing like Big Brother.	A B C D E
17.	We cannot know what is real. We can only believe what we think is real.	A B C D E
18.	The word 'real' has many meanings.	A B C D E
19.	Physical reality is the only reality. 'Emotional reality' or 'philosophical reality' are just like a soap bubble: catch them and they burst.	A B C D E
20.	I live my life by factual, genuine, actual reality, not by guesses, values or beliefs.	A B C D E
21.	I live my life by putting my beliefs into action. It's the only way to do it.	A B C D E

© 2008 RE Today Services
Permission is granted to photocopy this page for use in classroom activities in schools that have purchased this publication.

Four stories to explore 'the real'

Four ways to get yourself thinking. In a group of four, read one of the boxes each. Summarise it for the others. Discuss: What do these example say about reality? What questions would you like to get answered on this topic? Note them down.

Plato's parable of the cave

Two thousand five hundred years ago, the Greek Philosopher Plato wrote this: 'Imagine a group of prisoners caged in a cave from their births, all chained to the face the wall, with their backs to the cave's entrance. A fire burns behind them, and casts shadows onto the only wall they can see. The gaolers pass behind them and the fire behind them throws shadows onto the wall – of a "girl" or a "tree" or a "sword". All they ever see is shadows on the wall. These wretched prisoners think they know what the real world is, but it's all shadows. They recognise the shadows: "That's a tree," they say, "That's a horse," and in a sense this is true, but how little they know really! What would happen if one of them got out, and saw reality, and came back to tell them all about it?'

Well, Plato says they would kill him for a dangerous madman.

And Plato believes we are all like the prisoners. What we call 'real' is just 2D shadows compared to the pure world out there which Plato believed in.

Plato's parable was created to support his philosophy: that this world is a shadow of the real transcendent world of true, pure forms. Some people think the Matrix movie is based on the Platonic story.

Image © Focus Educational Images

A movie that messes with your head

In the film *The Matrix*, the world that we all think is real turns out to be an illusion. The freedom we feel we have is also an illusion. Forces from beyond our world can watch us, and affect us, for good or for evil. Our hero Neo lives within the Matrix, like us all, unknowing. But he escapes into the future. He asks his rescuers: 'Why are my eyes hurting?' They tell him: 'Because you've never used them before.' Neo returns to our world of illusions, coming into the world as we know it to create freedom. Opposed by the forces of evil and repression, he fights for freedom and in the end gives his life. But on the other side of death he lives again, and death can no longer hurt him. He finds his own freedom, and makes freedom for others too.

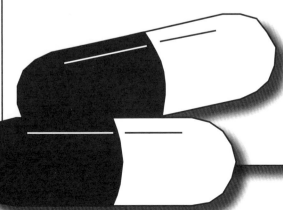

See a clip from *The Matrix*, or get students who know the movie to explain some key scenes.

Is our 'real world' just an illusion?

Is our sense of making free choices just a con? If it were, how would we know?

Some people say that *The Matrix* is inspired by Plato's parable of the c

Dreams and realities

It is early morning, still not yet quite light. You are lying in bed. You have been dreaming, but now you're awake. At least, you think you are. In your dream, the person you most want to be with was with you for the evening yesterday, was by your side, coming home with you. To your surprise, delight, you look across and there is that person, lying asleep beside you. You gaze in amazement. You scan your memory – nothing. As you look with love across in the dark room, you wonder if you are still dreaming. You think to yourself: If I reach out and touch the one I love, this spell will break. I will wake up. To speak might do the same. But it all feels so real. What to do? Do you speak, or touch?

Images provided by PhotoArt Vol 2

Yes

You reach across and touch. As you do so, s/he speaks first: 'Don't touch me. This is your dream speaking, and there's no touch in dreams. Keep the fantasy going.' You hesitate. What do you do next?

No

You stay quite still, enjoying the moment. It still feels totally dreamlike and unreal. You think: 'There is no sense of smell in a dream, but I can smell flowers and fresh coffee.' How can you decide if it is a dream, or real? What do you do next?

The Enlightened Chicken: a Buddhist story

Once there was a clever little chicken, growing up in an eggshell. She could feel her wings growing, her whole body getting bigger. She knew she was changing. She lived in the dark, in a tiny universe. Food supplies seemed to be running out, space was very tight. She was worried. Would she die if she ate the universe?

Then one day she felt a strong urge to break free. It was frightening, but exciting too. Where would this urge lead her? She was a courageous chick, so she followed the urge to be free and began to peck at the edge of her universe. Suddenly, the whole thing cracked open, the universe she had known literally split in two and she was in a brand new world – the outside world. Everywhere there was warmth, bright lights, sights to see. She looked around, felt her wings flap, took a deep breath of the warm spring air. Everything about her old life suddenly made sense. She felt wonderful!

She noticed other eggs in the nest she had come from: she was the first to hatch. She wondered about her brothers and sisters. They were still living in the dark; maybe they were as scared as she had been five minutes earlier. How could she tell them? She realised each chicken must find reality for themselves but she felt compassion for them, so while Mother Hen went to peck some grain, the chicken sat on the eggs for her, warming them and speeding the moment when her brothers and sisters would see reality for themselves.

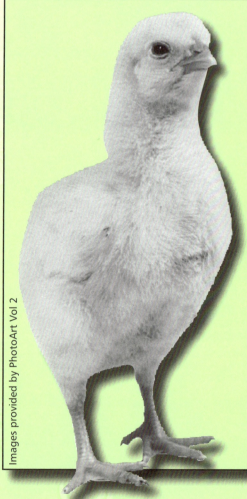

Images provided by PhotoArt Vol 2

What's real? Who says? A maze of ideas

This page of quotations and questions aims to start a discussion about questions of reality and religion.

> No one knows that they are not dreaming. You think I might be a part of your dream. You're wrong. I think you are all a part of my dream.

> Reality is a prison, where one vegetates and always will. All the rest, thought, action, is just a pastime, mental or physical. What counts then, is to come to grips with reality. The rest can go.
> *Cesare Pavese (1908–1950), Italian poet, novelist, translator*

> Reality is the name we give to our disappointments.
> *Mason Cooley (b.1927)*

> Love is the only reality and it is not a mere sentiment. It is the ultimate truth that lies at the heart of creation.
> *Rabindranath Tagore, Hindu Poet, Nobel prize winner (1861–1941)*

> I think the worst illusion of life is the illusion of freedom. I think I've chosen these clothes, this hairstyle, these shoes, but then I find that the big firms decided two years ago what the fashions and colours 16-year-olds would wear today were to be. Freedom – I feel free, but I'm not. The illusion sucks.

> Reality is merely an illusion, albeit a very persistent one
> *Albert Einstein (1879–1955)*

Image provided by PhotoArt Vol1

> The world, indeed, is like a dream and the treasures of the world are an alluring mirage! Like the apparent distances in a picture, things have no reality in themselves, but they are like heat haze.
> *Prince Gautama Siddharta, the founder of Buddhism, (563–483 BCE)*

> Life is one big road with lots of signs.
> So when you're riding through the ruts, don't complicate your mind.
> Flee from hate, mischief and jealousy.
> Don't bury your thoughts, put your vision to reality.
> Wake Up and Live!
> *Bob Marley, Jamaican reggae musician and Rasta hero (1945–1981)*

Four roles in the discussion:

A is the facilitator: Read out the questions, ask each person what they think in turn.

B is the cynic: Say some negative things about each quote.

C is the cheerleader: Say some positive things about each quote.

D is the writer: Make notes of all the ideas the group covers.

Reality bites

1. Which quotations are hard to understand? Can you agree on what they mean?

2. Some people say 'I only believe my senses'. Magic tricks, hallucinations and mirages are examples of our senses being unreliable. Swap your experiences of unreliable senses.

3. Which of the quotes do you think makes a good point?

4. Some religions teach that we are mostly in the dark about reality. What examples of this idea do you know?

5. As a group, produce a definition of reality. Allow another group to criticise it, and you work out what's wrong with theirs.

© 2008 RE Today Services
Permission is granted to photocopy this page for use in classroom activities in schools that have purchased this publication.

Does believing in God make people good?

'Without God, anything is allowable.'
(Dostoevsky)

For the teacher

This section sets out to encourage students in the 14–16 age group to explore the following questions, referring to Christianity, Buddhism and atheism:

- Are there links between morals and belief in God?
- Where do we get our moral values in a secular society?

The aim is to examine some of the factors that influence our moral awareness and consider ideas about links between belief in God and ethics.

Activity 1   A starter for thinking

The walking discussion sheet (page 11) begins to engage students with some fundamental questions about the significance of believing in God. It gives students an opportunity to see the diversity of attitudes amongst their own peers about the existence of God and any possible link between God and ethics. Ask for feedback in a brief class discussion after the task.

Activity 2   What did Dostoevsky mean by saying 'Without God, anything is allowable'?

Do we need God to have morals? Using Dostoyevsky's powerful quotation as a centre point, the aim is to encourage students to construct developed arguments running in diverse directions. By completing a thought development activity (page 12) around the statement, get students to enter into a discussion about the significance of this quotation:

- What does it mean?
- Is it a statement or a question?
- Is it true?
- Has it come true?
- Is society less religious/moral than when Dostoevsky wrote? How would we know?
- Is it something to be frightened of, or excited about?

Activity 3   Expressing views clearly

This extended writing activity enables students to draw on a variety of points of view, putting them into their own words and expressing their own personal evaluation. Use the PowerPoint presentation (on the website: www.retoday.org.uk) and/or the information sheet (page 13) on the attitudes of Christians, Buddhists, atheists and those of Dostoevsky and Nietzsche.

Arguments can be built up, with explanation, into a fully developed discussion of this philosophical issue using the multi-choice writing frame (page 12), creating a structure for an essay.

Learning objectives

- To explore the relationship between believing in God and ethical behaviour
- To ask and answer the question: do ethics need to have a transcendent origin?
- To develop an understanding of the foundation of our moral attitudes

Learning outcomes: Students will express informed arguments, making reference to differing views and beliefs. They will reflect on their own opinions, justifying them through use of reasoning and a developed vocabulary.

Most students will be able to give a view about whether our morals come from God or whether society creates its own values (level 4);

Many students will be able to explain two or more viewpoints about whether ethical systems can be developed by societies independently of any belief in a divine being. They will ask and respond to questions about whether society has becomes less moral if belief in God declines (level 5);

Some students will be able to analyse connections between belief in God, religious conformity and moral systems. They will be able to interpret the idea that different forms of belief create different ethical frameworks and that religion itself can be seen as a social construct (level 6).

Walking discussion activity

This activity uses statements to develop responses for discussion. Every student takes a copy and walks round. Talk briefly to someone about number 1, get their initials in the box that shows their view, and move on. Talk to someone else about number 2. Go twice through the sheet; get at least 18 other people to put their initials on your sheet, to show where their views go. Give them your views too. Notice the diversity in the group.

	Agree ←								→ Disagree	
1. There are no good reasons for believing in God.	1	2	3	4	5	6	7	8	9	10
2. God is a guiding power.	1	2	3	4	5	6	7	8	9	10
3. 'God' is an out-of-date idea and a dying word.	1	2	3	4	5	6	7	8	9	10
4. We have a sense for God deep inside our minds.	1	2	3	4	5	6	7	8	9	10
5. Atheists are just as moral as believers.	1	2	3	4	5	6	7	8	9	10
6. Society is less moral than it used to be.	1	2	3	4	5	6	7	8	9	10
7. Believing in God gives people a stronger sense of right and wrong.	1	2	3	4	5	6	7	8	9	10
8. Human beings created God. We made up the whole idea ourselves.	1	2	3	4	5	6	7	8	9	10
9. Ultimately, all morals come from God.	1	2	3	4	5	6	7	8	9	10

© 2008 RE Today Services
Permission is granted to photocopy this page for use in classroom activities in schools that have purchased this publication.

Engaging with secondary RE: Philosophical RE

Thinking about God and morality

Write comments in the boxes to help you explore what the statement might mean.

'Without God, anything is allowable.'

5. If God is a law-giver, then he would…

6. If there's no 'heavenly policeman' then…

7. What I think about the quote is…

8. An argument that supports this view is…

4. Some people disagree with the quote because…

9. Without any moral rules, humanity would…

3. Some people agree with the quote because…

1. What I think this means is…

I also want to say…

2. If there's no God, human beings would be free from…

Complete the sheet in a group of four, passing it on after you have filled in each section.

© 2008 RE Today Services
Permission is granted to photocopy this page for use in classroom activities in schools that have purchased this publication.

Does believing in God make people good?

Do we need to have God to have morals? Information sheet

Key question: As formal religion has declined in the West, have we become more moral, or less moral? How can you tell? Why?
This page sets out some ideas and arguments relating to the question.

Christian: For Christians, God is our creator; he has set out rules for people to live by. These form the foundation of how we should act. Through our conscience we can know God's laws and live a moral life. Having faith in a loving God means trusting that he has given us rules on how to live that will benefit us: God's laws give us guidance, showing us how to behave. Jesus said '**Love God** ... and **love your neighbour** as yourself.' Loving God is linked to our respect for each other. Christians also believe that the Holy Spirit of God can give people guidance and strength to do good and avoid evil.

Buddhist: Buddhists say that believing in God is not important. It makes no difference to our morality whether God exists or not. Living a moral life is important because it takes us on a path (dharma) to Enlightenment (nirvana), but morals don't come from God. The **Buddha** taught that debating about whether God exists is **not** a useful discussion; it does not help us to live better lives. We need to find our own path to enlightenment by **testing out** every rule we are told to follow, even if they are the rules taught by the Buddha himself! People should find skilful means to practise compassion as they journey to enlightenment.

Atheist: Atheists argue that God does not exist. They say that believing in a divine being is ignorant; it stops you asking questions and thinking for yourself. Human beings need to feel free to make mistakes without fear of being judged by a frightening deity. We can work out our own morals without worrying about heaven and hell. Atheists hold that rationality and honesty teach us what is good, not God.

Agnostic: Agnostics say that it is possible that a God or gods exist and so it would be wrong to reject the idea of a loving, divine being altogether. An agnostic would say that our morals may come from our beliefs in God, but we could make up our own morals too, influenced by the society we live in, those we admire and our own sense of goodness.

Dostoevsky: In 1880 the Russian author Dostoevsky wrote a book in which he questioned the link between God and morality. One of the main characters, Ivan, is an atheist, who believes that **'without God, anything is allowable'**. This seems to mean that in a world without God people can act just as they choose. Dostoevsky was asking a fundamental question: do we need to believe in God to have morals? Without a divine truth is there any reason to choose good over bad? Can a society that rejects God make up its own ethical rules? Can we all now behave just as we want to, which could be a recipe for moral chaos? By destroying God are we destroying goodness? Does goodness exist independently of God?

Nietzsche: Later in the 1880s, Nietzsche (a German philosopher) pronounced: **'God is Dead.'** By this he meant that God is an idea of the past, not the future. He believed that we must face the truth that there is no longer any value in believing in God, so **'anything now is imaginable'**. Nietzsche argued that we should make our own rules for ourselves, thinking freely without fear of God.

Engaging with secondary RE: Philosophical RE

Writing about God and morality
'Without God, anything is allowable'

With reference to the views of Buddhists, Christians and atheists, with additional comments inspired by the thinking of Nietzsche and Dostoevsky, all interpreted through your own understanding, use the boxes to create your essay. Choose at least two prompts from at least seven of the nine boxes (but be flexible). Complete them thoroughly for yourself, using the ideas from your lesson, research, discussions and the information sheet (page 13).

• My ideas about God… • People who believe in God… • No one knows… • When I think about God…	• Some people say… • History teaches us… • Nowadays… • People say that our rules come from…	• I'd like to know… • One thing that puzzles me is… • When we think about how to behave, we… • The thing that influences us most…
• Nietzsche would have said … • Human beings need to… • Trying to be an individual means … • If God is dead we can…	• Dostoevsky would say… • Maybe we still need God because… • The danger is that… • The thing that worries a lot of people is…	• An atheist might say… • By rejecting God… • True morals are… • You can be sure what is good by… • The really exciting thing now is…
• A Buddhist might argue… • The Buddha said… • A moral life for Buddhists means… • The path to enlightenment… • Because Buddhists don't believe in a God…	• Christians believe… • God is… • Christians say our morals… • Because God is the creator… • God speaks to us… • Jesus' example suggests…	• What I really think is… • In the end… • This makes me think… • I'm still wondering about… • We need the freedom to…

Why evil and suffering?

For the teacher

The tension between an all-loving, all-powerful, all-knowing deity and the reality of evil and suffering is profound. It is one of the main reasons offered by those who do not believe in God. Most people have something to say about this, often angry and heartfelt; pupils in the RE classroom are no exception.

The activities in this section are based around the philosophical concept of a 'valid argument'. An example of this, as an atheist may present it, goes like this:

1. **If** God desires something, and is able to accomplish it, then it will occur.
2. **If** God exists, he is all-good and all-powerful.
3. **If** God is all-good he would want to prevent all evil.
4. **If** God is all-powerful he would have the ability to prevent all evil.
5. **If** God wants to prevent all evil, and is able to accomplish it, then there would be no evil.
6. **Evil** exists.
7. **Therefore** God does not exist.

This is a valid argument (i.e. it makes no logical mistakes) but the fact that a significant percentage of the world's population claim allegiance to one religion or another suggests that there are challenges that can and must be made to this argument. Can pupils identify the premise most likely to succumb to challenge (it's number 5) and can they mount an effective and logical attack?

Approaching the subject in this way succeeds in introducing some welcome objectivity and rigour, and encourages the development of some important skills for good RE: analysis, deduction and clarification.

Activity 1 Analysing the argument

This activity introduces pupils to the formal expression of an argument, in order to encourage an objective and analytical approach to an emotive topic.

Provide pupils with a copy of **page 16**. Source A provides some background. In pairs, ask them to:

- **rank order** the seven statements to form a logical sequence, and **explain** their reasoning
- **decide** who might present an argument with this conclusion and **suggest** how Source B could be used to challenge their argument
- **identify** which of the premises (1–6) is most open to attack by the data in Source B
- **devise** a dialogue between a person who supports the premise identified above, and a person who wants to challenge it.

Activity 2 South Park: Cartmanland

The best contemporary expression of the argument about evil and suffering is found in series 5, episode 71 of South Park! This may not be your programme of choice (it's a '15', and rather rude), but it makes the necessary points extremely well. **See:** www.tv.com/south-park/cartmanland/episode/60546/summary.html.

Provide pupils with a copy of **page 17**. Read it with them, and then ask them in pairs to:

- **summarise** the main reason why Kyle loses his faith (part 1) in 25 words
- **identify** which premise is challenged by Kyle (part 2)
- **suggest** what other 'goods' could come from the suffering that Kyle and Cartman experience. Is it worth it? Are these convincing reasons?
- **hotseat** the three main characters, focusing on the challenge to premise 5.

Engaging with secondary RE: Philosophical RE

What makes a valid argument?

	If God is all-good he would want to prevent all evil.
	If God wants to prevent all evil, and is able to accomplish it, then there would be no evil.
	If God desires something, and is able to accomplish it, then it will occur.
	If God is all-powerful he would have the ability to prevent all evil.
	Evil exists.
	If God exists, he is all-good and all-powerful.
	Therefore God does not exist.

Source A

- **How is an argument set out?**

An argument is traditionally set out like this:
- **six** premises
- **one** conclusion.

- **What makes an argument valid?**

A valid argument makes **no logical mistake** (see the correct version of the argument above).

So ... **if** the premises (1–6) are true, **then** the conclusion (7) that God doesn't exist is also true.

- **Can a valid argument be challenged?**

Yes! Just because an argument is valid doesn't mean the conclusion is true! To challenge an argument you need to attack one or more of its premises.

Source B: Religion in Britain

UK population by religion, April 2001 (Census)

Religion	%
Christian	71.6
Buddhist	0.3
Hindu	1.0
Jewish	0.5
Muslim	2.7
Sikh	0.6
Other religion	0.3
All religions	**76.8**
No religion	15.5
Not stated	7.3
All no religion/not stated	**23.2**
Total	**100.00**

See: www.statistics.gov.uk

Images provided by Focus Educational Images

© 2008 RE Today Services
Permission is granted to photocopy this page for use in classroom activities in schools that have purchased this publication.

Why evil and suffering?

Does God exist? South Park investigates!

Source C: Cartmanland

Characters:

Eric Cartman: a very unpleasant character; the others are constantly making fun of him about his weight.

Kyle Broflovski: one of the few Jews in South Park, and Stan's best friend. The smartest of the four, he always learns from his mistakes.

Stan Marsh: an average, happy-go-lucky boy, and the leader of the gang. He almost always tries to do the right thing.

Kenny McCormick: the unlucky one. He is poor and lives in a run-down shack with his violent and drunken family.

Part 1

Cartman inherits $1million from his grandmother, whom he hated. This enables him to fulfil his lifelong dream of owning his own amusement park, 'Cartmanland'. He allows no one else to enter, and is the happiest person in the world.

When Kyle hears of Cartman's undeserved fortune, a painful haemorrhoid erupts in his backside. In his misery, he questions the very existence of God, and asks whether there is any reason to stay alive in a world where someone like Cartman is happy.

Kyle sees Cartman's happiness as a terrible evil which God would not allow if he existed. He loses his faith, and becomes an atheist.

Part 2

Cartman becomes miserable when he has to let other people into the park, and no longer has it to himself. He decides to sell it back to the original owners to get his money back, but the taxman and Kenny's family lay claim to the money.

Kyle is on his deathbed, having given up on life, but Stan takes him to see Cartman's misery. Stan says that God had only given Cartman the park so he could take it away from him and make him even more unhappy than he was before. Kyle looks up and says: 'Oh, so you *are* up there!'

Kyle quickly recovers both his health and his faith.

Suffering – is it worth it?

Activity 3 Theodicies continuum

Activities 3 and 4 invite pupils to engage with five commonly held theodicies (justifications of God in the face of evil and suffering). The question is asked: Are there any benefits of suffering that God is aware of and that justify the amount of suffering needed to achieve them? Put cards numbered 1–10 in a line on one wall of the room and provide a copy of the continuum response sheet for each pupil. Pupils then:

- **Make a private response** to the five statements; choose and mark the closest to their view. Fold it over twice.
- **Swap their response sheet** with others in the class. Pass the paper three times, so that no one really knows who has got which sheet. For the rest of the activity they represent the point of view expressed on the sheet they end up with (i.e. not their own).
- **As the teacher reads out each question**, pupils move to the number indicated on the sheet for that question, producing a 'living bar graph'.
- **Identify one question** where the responses were at different extremes of the continuum. Pupils representing each response plan key arguments for their position, and then seek to persuade the other groups of pupils to change their position.
- **Record** their current viewpoint by moving to the appropriate number on the continuum: note any shifts of opinion.

Suffering – is it worth it?   Female/Male

| Strongly disagree | 1 | 2 | 3 | 4 | 5 | 6 | Strongly agree |

1. Suffering is necessary because it allows human beings to show love and compassion.
2. Suffering is God's way of punishing sin.
3. Suffering is necessary if people are to have free will, and choose for themselves.
4. Suffering is justified because without it people wouldn't be able to appreciate goodness.
5. Suffering is needed for people to learn about the important things in life.

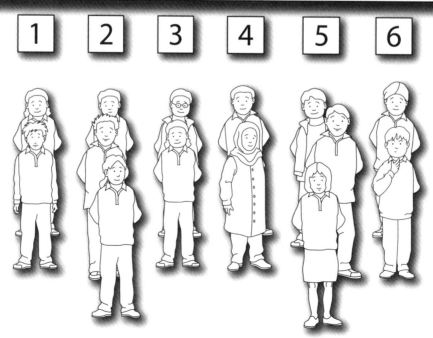

Why evil and suffering?

Activity 4 Pass the theodicy

Work in pairs – you will need a large sheet of A3 paper.

- **Choose** one source from D to H. You have five minutes to begin a **draft** response to the source: you might agree, disagree, raise questions, make comments.
- When your time is up, **swap** your paper with another group. **Continue** on their paper. You might redraft parts, delete points, add your own ideas.
- Repeat this several times, and then return the paper to the original owners, who will **produce a final version** of the response to the source.

Source D

Showing love and compassion

'I have always wanted to be a doctor but I don't know if it is my vocation. I like the idea of helping people on a daily basis, but I would also like to do some charity work throughout my life, working for a charity like Christian Aid or Oxfam.'

Female, aged 15

Source E

Punishing sin

'Pain and suffering is God's way of punishing those who do bad things. It is only fair that they be punished, but what I don't understand is why it is that so many innocent people suffer, rather than just those who have done wrong. That doesn't seem fair to me.'

Male, aged 13

Source F

Enjoying free will

'People say that God plans our future. If he did, he wouldn't be a very good God because babies, kids and innocent people die, and if he planned our future then why does he kill them? I believe he only gives us two paths, bad and good, and we choose from there.'

Male, aged 14

Source G

Appreciating goodness

'I want a world where we do not have wars and mass killing and where humans do not bully each other ... but I want a bit of bad because otherwise what would good be?'

Male, aged 12

Source H

Learning from suffering

Heather was diagnosed with spinal cancer when she was 17. After much reflection she concluded: 'There's got to be something that's controlling the universe. He gave me cancer for a reason: to make me a better person and to get through it.'

BBC Curriculum Bites: Challenging Beliefs, 14–16.

What is God like?

For the teacher

Ultimate questions often include questions about the existence and nature of God. This work enables pupils in the 11–14 age range to deepen their understanding of ideas about God. This links with themes of the English *Non-Statutory National Framework for RE:* 'key ideas and questions of meaning in religions and beliefs, including issues related to God'.

Achievements expressed as 'I can...' statements:

Level 3: I can...

- **Describe** two different ways in which people see God
- **Describe** my own ideas about God
- **Identify the impact** of respecting God's name.

Level 4: I can ...

- **Show that I understand** links between the behaviour of different religious groups and their ideas about God.

Level 5: I can...

- Use philosophical words and metaphor to **explain some similarities and differences** in the images of God that various religions use.

Resources

- http://www.arthafez.com/index.htm – Beautiful colour calligraphy and explanation of the 99 names of God in Islam.
- www.natre.org.uk/spiritedarts – Superb collections of pupils' artwork for RE on the theme 'Where is God?'
- www.thechurchofyhwh.org/GINGN/gingn.htm – Christian site with very user-friendly unpacking of the meanings behind the name of God in Jewish and Christian scripture.
- www.mp3raid.com/search/mp3/gloria_gaynor.html pg2 'I am what I am.' Download the music file: it needs Windows Media Player or RealPlayer.

For information

- Judaism, Christianity and Islam are monotheistic religions: they believe that there is only one God. Jews and Muslims place much importance on the oneness and unity of God. Although Christians also believe in the oneness of God this is sometimes misunderstood, because Christians believe that the one God is triune (the Holy Trinity): God the Father, God the Son and God the Holy Spirit. For Christians this is not a denial of monotheism but expresses the profundity of the nature of God.

- 'God' is such a complex idea that if we ask what God is like we will probably hear something different from each person. Hundreds of different images seek to explain the nature of God, who he really is, what he is like and what kind of qualities he possesses. Is the truth in none of these, or all of them taken together? Are some images of God incompatible with others?

- Christianity and Judaism share some of the same personal images of God, but Islam rejects this kind of personification of God as wrong. Instead Muslims concentrate on Allah's attributes.

- Muslims believe in the Oneness of God – Tawhid – that there is only one God and that he is one being. Muslims believe that God is different from anything the human mind can think of or imagine. They believe we should try to understand the attributes of God that do not require us to make any mental pictures of him.

Ideas for adapting this work

To include more 'learning from religion', download Gloria Gaynor's song 'I am what I am'. Play it as pupils enter the classroom. Consider: What am I like? In groups, pupils write the name of each person in their group (including themselves) on a piece of paper. They then write as many *positive* comments as they can about each person. Give them about two minutes per person. Each person in turn hears the comments about them from everyone. The pupil concerned writes out 'I am...' and then copies out the comments about themselves. Discussion can follow if they did not think anyone had seen them the way they saw themselves.

What is God like?

What's in a name?

Activity
Take the 24 names of Allah given below and cut them into individual cards. In fours, turn them over one at a time: what information does each card give you about the Muslim understanding of Allah? Is there anything surprising about each one? If you were introducing the Muslim understanding of Allah to a class of small children – say those half your age – which six names would you choose to start with? Why?

Choose three of the names:
The one you think **best sums** up what God is like

The one you find hardest to understand

The one you think is **most surprising** or unusual

Write these up with your reasons for choosing them.

Al-Fattah The Opener	*Al-Alim* The Knower of All	*As-Salam* The Source of Peace
Al-Muhaymin The Guardian	*Al-Ghaffar* The Forgiving	*As-Sami* The Hearer of All
Al-Karim The Generous	*Al-h Haqq* The Truth	*Al-Qadir* The All Powerful
As-Sabur The Patient One	*Al-Hadi* The Guide	*An-Nur* The Light
Al-Mani The Preventer of Harm	*Al-Wali* The Protecting Friend	*Al-Barr* The Doer of Good
Al-Awwal The First	*Al-Mumit* The Taker of Life	*Al-Akhir* The Last
Al-Matin The Forceful One	*Al-Mu'akhkhir* The Delayer	*Ad-Darr* The Creator of the Harmful
Al-Ahad The One	*Al-Wajid* The Finder	*Al-Muqit* The Nourisher

© 2008 RE Today Services
Permission is granted to photocopy this page for use in classroom activities in schools that have purchased this publication.

Images and metaphors about God

Activity 1

Most of the time believers picture God as a person, even though they believe that God is spirit. Often the picture is of an old man who sits in the sky. Britney Spears once said she thought God had a 'long, white beard' and 'wanders around' in heaven (Doh!). Sometimes we use images and metaphors and say God is like something. The most common image or metaphor for God is that of Father. Others include rock, ruler, king and shepherd. **How many more can you think of?**

Activity 2

1. **What is God like?** In one or two words describe an image or metaphor you have for God.

   If you were an advertising agency 'selling God' how would you do it? Think up a 'God' campaign.

2. **Highlighting:** Brainstorm/write all the images, characteristics or metaphors for God you can on a large piece of paper, then highlight in one colour all that are found in Islam and in another colour those in Christianity. How many have two colours? Why is this, and what is its importance?

Activity 3

Here are four descriptions of what God might be like.

- **Read** them through and **summarise** them. Which one do you agree with?
- What kind of God does the writer believe in?
- These descriptions are of the pictures on the next page (and in colour on the RE Today/NATRE websites).
- Can you **match them together?** Summarise the pictures.
- Which picture do you like the most? Why?
- What questions would you like to ask the artist?
- Create your own image on the theme 'Searching for God'.

'The earth is a prison between heaven and hell. Earth is like a prison because there's always suffering. The only way out is dying. In my religion, the only way to God is to be good and pray. I personally think spiritual life is all about your intentions and prayers. If you intend to do good, that means you are a good person. The only way out of Earth's prison is by dying and entering eternal life.'

'I believe God is everywhere. Unlike many people, I don't believe he is the cause of anything. Our actions have consequences and we have to take responsibility, good or bad. God has nothing to do with it. I think God is more of a protector, a comfort, who people can turn to for help or advice through their religion. And it does help if you have someone to blame your mistakes on even though you have to face up to them one day.'

I thought of the story called 'Footprints in the Sand'. This story is represented in my artwork by a man. All the bad things that could go wrong in life have happened to him. The grim reaper stands for death. The lady is his wife, shouting, as they go through a divorce. The boy is his son. He is a heroin addict, slowly killing himself. The starving anorexic girl is the man's daughter. The broken credit card stands for his gambling debts. God, a figure in shining light, holds on to the man in all his troubles, the colour of hope.

'Many different religions talk about God. They all have their own special name: God, Allah, Yahweh, Haile-Selase and Brahman They all say God is the one Supreme Being, creator and ruler of the universe. This leads you to believe that he or she is in the clouds somewhere. Right?

But what if that's not true? What if God is on earth? What if God could be split into a million different forms at the same time? What if God was a woman, child, dog or cat? That's what I would call the Supreme Being: someone who is there for everyone, always. I believe you are never more than 15 feet away from a "God".'

What do you think these pictures are saying about God?

The community of philosophical enquiry: how can RE benefit?

In what ways is RE philosophical?

For the teacher: What is a philosophical question?

Philosophical questions are always controversial. They provoke conversation and create a degree of dissonance. There may not be clear answers to philosophical questions; we may have to be content with only making progress in our understanding of the scope of a question. Philosophical questions in the context of the community of enquiry must always be relevant to the community. It is essential that the questions come from the learners. They come from a shared area of concern and the question chosen for a particular enquiry will be chosen by the learners themselves. Philosophical questions are timeless and relate to the shared experience of humanity. This links philosophical question with the key areas of religious concern and is why philosophy and religion are often engaged with the same questions.

Types of thinking in the community of philosophical enquiry

In the community of philosophical enquiry we aim to cultivate skilful thinkers. These thinkers think:

- in creative ways and imaginative ideas
- in critical ways making, reasoned judgements
- in caring ways, sensitive to the views of others
- with others in community in a collaborative way.

For the teacher: What is a philosophical question?

Philosophy for Children (P4C) is underpinned by a desire to advance what could be called the 'virtue' of Reasonableness. This is not simply being able to reason, or to be rational. Reasonableness combines sound thinking with clear conceptualisation and ultimately forms people able to make strong ethical decisions and live well.

First, it is a process advancing skills of logical, hypothetical and inferential reasoning, e.g. 'does it always follow that...?' 'What if...?' 'Could you give an example...?' 'If ....is true then what follows?'

Second, it is a process developing philosophical conceptualisation. A community of enquiry is philosophical when the teacher/facilitator encourages students to take the enquiry deeper into the ideas raised. The teacher must be able to recognise a philosophical idea when it comes up. RE teachers often have good understanding here. Philosophical concepts include justice, love, responsibility, freedom, friendship, what it means to be human, hope and God.

Third, this process helps young people form values which will guide their lives. The community of philosophical enquiry helps students investigate and make reasoned judgements with their peers about what kind of people they want to be and what kind of a world they want to live in.

Pupils enjoy the community of enquiry as it puts their views on the level with others.

How can RE benefit?

What students tell us about the community of philosophical enquiry when exploring questions like 'What does it mean to be human?'

'I prefer to be in an enquiry because it is more enjoyable and more arguments develop because everyone involved in this is good when discussing a subject like this as we hear everyone's point of view.'
Tom, 14

'I think a good way to work is in the community of enquiry because we tend to understand each other better as we see all who may speak.'
Paige, 13

'I think a good way to work is in the community of enquiry because every one gets a chance to speak in turn and it's more relaxed and you feel more involved with different arguments.'
Bryony, 14

'...because we can see people when they talk and I feel that it gets the point across easier if you can see the person who is talking.'
Josh, 13

'...because everyone has their own say and listens and thinks more because other people are saying what they think. You want to disagree and have your say and it helps to develop your ideas.'
Lauren, 14

'...because then we can work together to find out what everybody thinks...'
Eliot, 13

'In a philosophical enquiry you get to hear other people's points of view. There are lots of voices in the world, and in an enquiry you get to hear some of them. Maybe you even change your mind about an idea in a way you hadn't thought of before.'
Jess, 13

Links to useful websites:

SAPERE is the UK-wide organisation co-ordinating the community of philosophical enquiry. The 'links' page has a comprehensive selection of links to interesting worldwide sites. The website offers links to international journals, current research and reflections regarding P4C. www.sapere.net

Institute for the Advancement of Philosophy for Children: The IAPC provides curriculum materials for engaging young people in philosophical enquiry: http://cehs.montclair.edu/academic/iapc Based at Montclair Steve University in the USA, it is where Matthew Lipman began and developed his work.

The International Council of Philosophical Inquiry with Children (ICPIC) was created in 1985 networking teachers and educators from around the world interested in engaging children in communities of philosophical enquiry. http://www.icpic.org/

Thinking Worlds is a website devoted to developing the community of philosophical enquiry, supporting education for sustainable development and education for intercultural understanding. www.thinkingworlds.org:

The European Foundation for the Advancement of Doing Philosophy with Children: http://sophia.eu.org/

Structure of the community of philosophical enquiry: ten steps

Step 1 – Clarify the broad field of enquiry with the group: For example, ethics (questions about how we decide what actions are right or wrong), medical ethics (questions about the value of life and prioritising human over other life), aesthetics (questions about beauty), philosophy of religion (questions about the nature of God).

Step 2 – Present a stimulus: story, photo, video clip, or perhaps an activity that creates some conflicting views or opinions. From this come some questions of a philosophical nature. The questions can be formulated individually, in pairs or in small groups.

Step 3 – Collect questions: The questions are written up for the whole class to see.

Step 4 – Select a main question: The questions are discussed, and one chosen by the community and not the teacher, usually through a vote of some sort. In this way the broad field of enquiry is now focused down onto something much more precise: philosophy works towards more precise and clear thinking about a complex issue of human concern.

Step 5 – Prepare for the enquiry: If possible, and there is a gap of time between choosing the question and the enquiry time itself, the teacher/facilitator can consider some lines that the enquiry could take. For example, if the question were something like 'Do all people have souls?', the teacher may bring some research on different views of the soul to support the learning.

Step 6 – Open the community of enquiry: Invite contributions from the group. Encourage students to build on each other's ideas by beginning their contributions with 'I think... because...' or 'I agree with ... because...' or 'I disagree with ... because...'.

Step 7 – Move towards forming a first hypothesis: '...maybe...' The facilitator can ask the group to think of ways in which it would be possible to confirm or otherwise the suggested hypothesis – for instance by the giving of examples and counter-examples.

Step 8 – Review the hypothesis: How far have we got with the question so far? How are we doing towards answering the question?

Step 9 – Consider another possibility or hypothesis: What are the alternative views?

Step 10 – Close the enquiry by making a philosophical judgement. Making a clear ending to the enquiry is very important. Some way of inviting students to consider how the enquiry has affected their thinking and may influence their lives is essential. This could be simply inviting students to raise a hand if they have had a new idea or seen a new viewpoint. Alternatively set a piece of research homework to find out more about something that came up in the conversation. Sometimes it will be possible to give more time to the enquiry if the students still have a great deal to unpack in the question.

What does it mean to be human? Two examples

> When designing a sequence of lessons to include the community of philosophical enquiry, it is important for the teacher to consider what philosophical concepts are anticipated to be explored in that sequence of lessons. GCSE and other RS courses give opportunities where philosophical concepts of the nature of humanity will be raised.

Example 1 Sanctity of Life

The topic of 'the sanctity of life' occurs in most GCSE courses. The possibility of the holiness or special status of human over other life is clearly a religious and philosophical concept. It applies to the area of human and animal rights, abortion and euthanasia, and is rich for the community of philosophical enquiry. In this example students had completed written work with the classroom arranged in regular rows. Students then moved into friendship groups to develop philosophical questions. While representatives from the groups were writing their questions on the board, the whole class were writing all the questions into their 'Philosophy Journals'. Examples of philosophical questions from students in a mixed ability class of 13–14s were:

- Is a fertilised egg a human being?
- What do we mean by human?
- If a baby with a handicap is aborted, does this mean disabled people are not accepted in our society?
- Is all life worthwhile?
- Who should decide the rights and wrongs on matters of medical ethics?
- Does the mother have the right to take away the child's life?
- What is normal?
- How old is a child conceived through IVF when the embryo has been frozen for some years?
- When does life begin?
- How would you feel if you discovered your embryo had been frozen for some years?
- Are we building towards a perfect race, like the Nazis?

Having considered the questions, the students voted for one to discuss in the next lesson. Working in this way over time, class communities become better able to judge which will be good questions for the enquiry. A complex multi-clause question may present difficulties in clarifying many definitions. The question this class chose for their enquiry was 'What is normal?'

Comments on the question before the enquiry

Students reflected on the question before the enquiry:

> 'I think this is a good question for enquiry because it is short, simple and has many possibilities. I think it will be interesting to see how people think.'
> *Hannah*

> 'people judge people as normal, but everyone is different.'
> *Emma*

> 'I think there is no such thing as normal and we are all different and we should accept each other for who and what they are. We should embrace others e.g. other religions and learn more before we judge if they are normal or not.'
> *Josh*

This enquiry raised many questions relating to the adolescent journey. The fact that students of this age chose this question was very interesting. There is much peer pressure to be 'normal' and in the community they were able to open the idea of normality up fully.

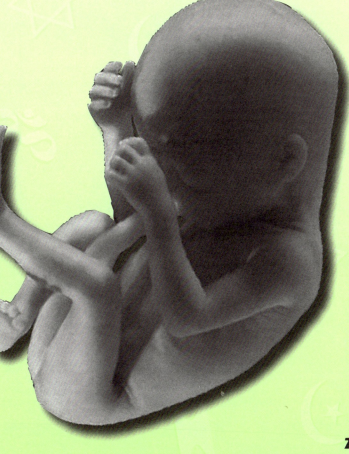

Image provided by PhotoArt Vol 1

Thoughts after the enquiry:

'I think the question we chose was a difficult question because different people think that normal is different things...'

Josh

'I think the question we chose was a good question because it could never be answered. It is like "Which came first, the chicken or the egg?" since there are so many different views on the question like: "There is no such thing as normal" and "we are all normal" and "nobody is normal". ... I think we need another enquiry to explore this question further.'

Matthew

'You can't say disabled people are normal or not normal, we should all be equal. Normal should not exist because it makes people feel cast away from others.'

Ailsa

This question was interesting for these Year 9 students as they are struggling personally to work out who they are and how they should behave. There is an idea of normality they feel pressurised into being, but through this enquiry the class discovered that normality is an illusion. We tried to clarify criteria for what would count as normal ... but very soon found that this was impossible. These questions opened up an exploration of the bigger area of 'What does it mean to be human?' as it helped students realise that the philosophical concept of 'human' was a very wide one.

Working with these questions supported the following lessons when we went on to consider in more detail issues about abortion and euthanasia. This is because a deeper level of thinking had been kindled about the core issues lying behind everything relating to medical ethics. We have discovered also that students of 13 can think deeply about these issues. The capacity of young people for philosophical reflection is a constant revelation. Boys who are normally not engaged or interested to write much at this stage contribute deeply to the enquiry. We have a hunch that in two years when they are in Year 11 they will also be writing well.

Example 2   Science and Religion

Questions around 'What does it mean to be human?' will develop in the topic 'Science and Religion'.

Students had been exploring the origins of the earth and humanity using various source material. As a stimulus to develop questions for the enquiry, students had taken a double page and explored the Genesis 2 story. The Tree was drawn in the middle of a double page. On the left, students were invited to draw the experience of Adam and Eve before they had eaten the apple and on the right of the page students explored the experience of Adam and Eve after eating the apple. Students were asked whether they would prefer to live as Adam and Eve before or after eating the fruit and to say why. Explorations of innocence and what it means to know (responsibility and so on) were made. Students were then asked to get into small groups to generate questions in the usual way.

Examples of questions generated through this were:

- 'Why are we bothered (about anything: the universe, school, money)?'
- 'What does it all mean?'
- 'Is God in space or in the sky?'
- 'Is it always good to know everything?'
- 'Does knowing something make you responsible?'
- 'Is the universe in balance?'

Image provided by PhotoArt Vol 1

Explore science and religion to challenge the idea of 'science versus religion'.

Is it true? How do you know? Some models of philosophical and religious truth

For the teacher

Some of the very best RE asks learners not only to examine the truth claims made by different religions but also to develop their own way of seeing reality in the light of these. Religion is, in one sense, a way of seeking the truth about life's mysteries. RE has not done its job just by exploring festivals without philosophy or looking at vestments but not verification. Philosophical RE should be space to enjoy asking bold questions: 'So which religion is right then?' 'They can't all be true can they?' The activities in this section give learners opportunities to evaluate the pictures of reality that different religions offer and reflect on their own perception of truth. The activities are designed for students in the 13–16 age range. This piece of work also links to the themes of beliefs and concepts and interfaith issues from the QCA's *Non-Statutory National Framework for RE*, and to key topics in GCSE and Standard Grade syllabuses.

For information

There are many different religions, each claiming to have the truth. Evaluating different descriptions of reality is part of RE. Does one religion have all the truth? Is the truth absolute? Or is it relative: do all religions lead to God? We believe things are true because we have seen them happen before. We believe things are true based on a theory developed by observation of other things. We believe they are true because they are true by definition. We may believe things are true because they fit well with other true things. To believe that there is only one truth, for all times and places, is called **absolutism**. To believe that truth is only defined between people, and truth can change in different times and places, is called **relativism**.

Pupils can show their achievements in terms of levels. These 'I can...' statements describe achievements in terms of levels 4–8. I can...

Level 4

- Show that I understand two different ways of looking at the truth.
- Apply the idea of truth to my own experience and point of view about a religious question.

Level 5

- Recognise and explain different religious and non-religious beliefs about truth.
- Express my own views about how we know the truth.

Level 6

- Use reasoning to express my own and others' insights into questions of truth.
- Present a coherent argument about different interpretations of questions of meaning and truth.

Level 7

- Use a wide religious and philosophical vocabulary in presenting a clear personal and critical evaluation of how people express their understanding of the truth in a variety of ways.

Level 8

- Analyse and account for different interpretations of religious expression and truth.
- Give an informed, contextualised and well-argued account of my own conclusions.

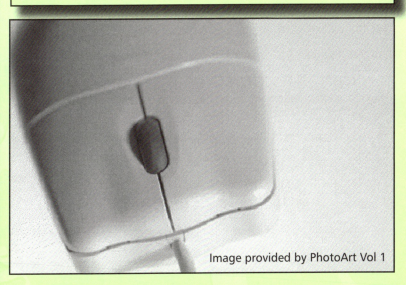

Image provided by PhotoArt Vol 1

Engaging with secondary RE: Philosophical RE

Activity for pupils

'"What is truth?" asked jesting Pilate, and did not stay for an answer.'

Francis Bacon, quoting John's Gospel

'We both have truths: are mine the same as yours?'

Pilate to Jesus, *Jesus Christ Superstar*

 There is a PowerPoint presentation to go with this article on the RE Today website, which includes some analysis of this activity.

www.retoday.org.uk

- First **sort** the statements below into those that are true and those that are not.
- **Explain** how you know. Which ones are difficult to answer? Why?
- Now sort them into **facts and opinions**. Is there a difference? Are there some you just cannot know?
- How can we judge whether our beliefs are true? Can we test our views with logic, argument, experience, discussion, consistency, history? Are there any other tests?

Arsenal are the best.	There is a Loch Ness monster.	God is real.
Dogs are better than cats.	Tony Blair was a British prime minister.	If a tree falls down in the forest, but no one is there, it makes no sound.
Triangles have three sides.	Ice is always cold.	All sheep have four legs.
The world is round.	The Battle of Hastings was in 1066.	It snows in winter.
Red is a colour.	Your teacher's front door is brown.	It will rain tomorrow.
1 + 5 = 6	Classical music helps cows produce more milk.	Jogging is bad for you.

REtoday Services

Is it true? How do you know?

Four ways of looking at the truth

Can you make sense of the images? Write captions or speech bubbles for each one

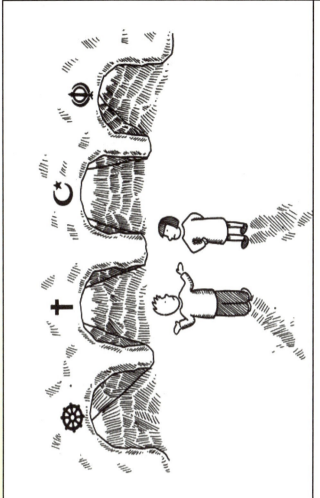

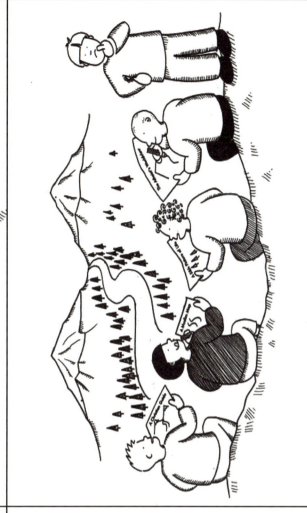

Drawings by Sophie Hardwicke ©RE Today

© 2008 RE Today Services
Permission is granted to photocopy this page for use in classroom activities in schools that have purchased this publication.

Engaging with secondary RE: Philosophical RE

Four descriptions of truth

These four descriptions of ideas about truth correspond to the pictures on the previous page. Match them up.

Mountain climbers? Some people think religions are like ways of climbing the mountain of life. There are several paths, each has its own charms and problems, but if you get on a path that leads onwards and upwards, you'll reach the truth at last. So people climbing the mountain get a bit closer to the truth as they get nearer the top. There is one truth, but different paths approach the truth in different ways. Of course some mountaineers fall off. Some find their path weaves back down again. Some never make it to the top. **This picture of religions says some may be 'more true' than others, but there is one truth, at the summit, where we all meet. The trouble is, we only get to the summit after we die!**

Elephant fondlers? In a popular poem, blind people feel an elephant, and go away with completely different (but all partly correct) ideas about what the elephant is like. The poem points out that our perceptions of the truth might be very incomplete: we don't know it all! Some people might explain the differences between religions like this: Different religions have each 'got hold' of a different part of the truth about God. **This picture of religion says they are all a bit true, but mostly wrong in their description of reality. The disagreements between religions happen because all human ideas about God are incomplete and just part of the picture.**

Map readers? Some people think religious people are like map makers or map readers. The religions offer a map, and can guide you. But you won't really know if your map was good and accurate until you reach the end of the journey. The Christian map, for example, shows a way to heaven. But what if you arrive, and find there's no such place? The Hindu map says the best end of human life is found in Moksha. But is it so? Muslims teach that Allah will judge you when you die. But can it be proved? **This picture of religions says that in some ways everyone has to draw their own map for the journey of life as they go along.**

Tunnel dwellers? This picture suggests that each religion is like a tunnel out of the underground caverns of life, a way to the bright outside. But when you begin, you can't tell if the tunnel leads out. You have to guess, or choose, or follow someone's advice. And if you spend your whole life struggling up a tunnel, and find it's a dead end, it seems a big waste. **This picture might see all religions, or many religions, as leading out of the dark into the light. Or maybe there's only one way out. We can't be sure.**

Activity for pupils

1. Using the pictures on page 31, work in groups of four to answer these questions:
   - Describe what is going on in each of the pictures.
   - What does this suggest about the truth?
   - What does this suggest about religions and truth?
   - What else would you like to ask about the picture?
   - What do you think of this example of a way of deciding what is true?
2. Using the descriptions above, match them to the correct pictures.
3. How can we know the truth about the religious questions?
4. Rank the four views of truth: which does your group think is best? Which is least useful? Are they 'true'?
5. Are there any religions you think are absolutist about the truth?